Grocer

Jeff Barger

Rourke
Educational Media
rourkeeducationalmedia.com

A Division of
Carson Dellosa
Education

BEFORE AND DURING READING ACTIVITIES

Before Reading: *Building Background Knowledge and Vocabulary*

Building background knowledge can help children process new information and build upon what they already know. Before reading a book, it is important to tap into what children already know about the topic. This will help them develop their vocabulary and increase their reading comprehension.

Questions and Activities to Build Background Knowledge:

1. Look at the front cover of the book and read the title. What do you think this book will be about?
2. What do you already know about this topic?
3. Take a book walk and skim the pages. Look at the table of contents, photographs, captions, and bold words. Did these text features give you any information or predictions about what you will read in this book?

Vocabulary: *Vocabulary Is Key to Reading Comprehension*

Use the following directions to prompt a conversation about each word.
- Read the vocabulary words.
- What comes to mind when you see each word?
- What do you think each word means?

Vocabulary Words:
- *pallets*
- *produce*
- *register*
- *stock*

During Reading: *Reading for Meaning and Understanding*

To achieve deep comprehension of a book, children are encouraged to use close reading strategies. During reading, it is important to have children stop and make connections. These connections result in deeper analysis and understanding of a book.

 Close Reading a Text

During reading, have children stop and talk about the following:
- Any confusing parts
- Any unknown words
- Text to text, text to self, text to world connections
- The main idea in each chapter or heading

Encourage children to use context clues to determine the meaning of any unknown words. These strategies will help children learn to analyze the text more thoroughly as they read.

When you are finished reading this book, turn to the next-to-last page for an **After Reading Activity**.

Table of Contents

Community Helpers

Community helpers are all around us.
They make our lives better.

People who live or work in the same area are part of a community.

What Does a Grocer Do?

A grocer is a community helper.

Grocers sell food at a grocery store.

Grocery stores also sell items such as paper towels.

Big trucks bring food to the store.

Workers unload boxes of food.

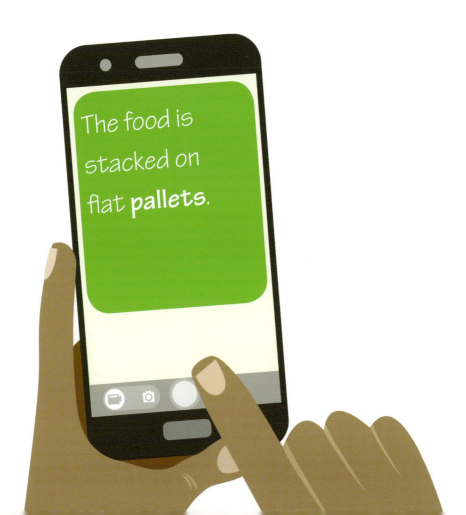

The food is stacked on flat **pallets**.

Grocers **stock** food on shelves. They help customers find what they need.

Grocers sell fresh vegetables to customers.

Around the Store

Fruits and vegetables are called **produce**.

Each group of food has a place in the store.

PRODUCE SPECIAL
MANGOES
MEXICO GROWN
98¢ EA

PRODUCE SPECIAL
ORGANIC SUGAR PLUM TOMATOES
$2.77

PRODUCE SPECIAL
ORGANIC
CANTALOUPE
MEXICO GROWN
$2.87 EA

13

Special shelves keep some produce cold.

Cold produce stays fresh.

The deli has hot and cold food.
Meats and cheeses are sold here.

Grocers give customers small bites to try. These are called samples.

It is time to pay.

A clerk will take your money.

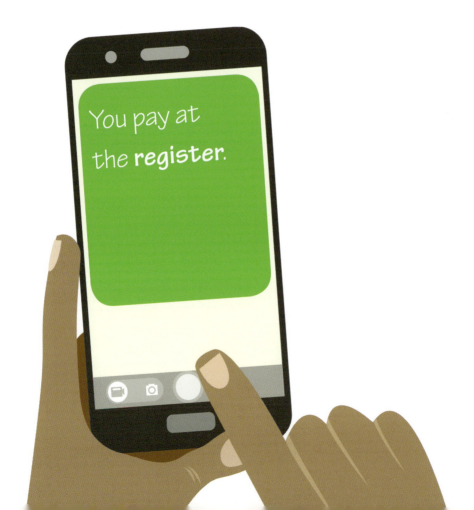

You pay at the **register**.

19

We need food every day.

Grocers make sure it is ready for us.

Activity

Let's Go Shopping!

Supplies
- paper
- pencil
- markers
- computer and printer
- tape or glue

You can help your family shop for groceries. The first step is to make a list. Include all the things your family will need for the next few days.

Directions
1. Write the names of ten items your family will need in the next few days.
2. Draw a picture of each item. Or, print out a picture of each item and tape or glue it beside its name.
3. Take the list when you go to the grocery store. Cross out each item as you put it in the cart.

Photo Glossary

 **pallets** (PAL-its): Flat, hard platforms used for stacking and moving things.

 **produce** (PROH-doos): Things that are produced or grown for eating, especially fruits and vegetables.

 **register** (REJ-i-stur): A machine that automatically records and counts.

 **stock** (stahk): To gather and keep a supply of a product to sell.

Index

After Reading Activity

Ask an adult to help you collect food packages after your family has finished using them. Make sure to empty boxes and to rinse out bottles and jars. Then, use the packages to make your own grocery store. Put prices on your items. Invite family members and friends to shop at your store.

About the Author

Jeff Barger is an author, blogger, and literacy specialist. He lives in North Carolina. He likes to shop at grocery stores that have free samples!

www.rourkeeducationalmedia.com

Edited by: Kim Thompson
Cover and interior design by: Kathy Walsh

Photo Credits: Cover, title page, p.11, 20, 22: ©XiXinXing; p.5: ©Rawpixel.com; p.7: ©asiseeit; p.9, 22: ©PierreDesrosiers; p.13, 22: ©Bill Oxford; p.15: ©baranozdemier; p.17: ©leaf; p.19, 22: ©andresr

Library of Congress PCN Data

Grocer / Jeff Barger
(Community Helpers)
ISBN 978-1-73161-423-0 (hard cover)(alk. paper)
ISBN 978-1-73161-218-2 (soft cover)
ISBN 978-1-73161-528-2 (e-Book)
ISBN 978-1-73161-633-3 (ePub)
Library of Congress Control Number: 2019932040

Rourke Educational Media
Printed in the United States of America,
North Mankato, Minnesota